Here Is the Tropical Rain Forest

Madeleine Dunphy

ILLUSTRATED BY

Michael Rothman

HYPERION BOOKS FOR CHILDREN

NEW YORK

Printed in Singapore.
For more information address
Hyperion Books for Children,
114 Fifth Avenue, New York, New York 10011.

FIRST EDITION
3 5 7 9 10 8 6 4 2

Library of Congress Cataloging-in-Publication Data

Dunphy, Madeleine.
Here is the tropical rain forest/Madeleine Dunphy; illustrated by Michael Rothman—1st ed.
    p.   cm.
Summary: Cumulative text presents the animals and plants of the tropical rain forest and their relationship
with one another and their environment.
ISBN 1-56282-636-0 (trade)—1-56282-637-9 (lib. bdg.)
1. Rain forest ecology—Juvenile literature. 2. Rain forest fauna—Juvenile literature. 3. Rain forest plants—
Juvenile literature. 4. Rain forests—Juvenile literature. [1. Rain forest animals. 2. Rain forest plants. 3. Rain
forest ecology. 4. Ecology.] I. Rothman, Michael, ill. II Title.
QH541.5.R27D85   1994
574.5'2642'0913—dc20   93-24850 CIP   AC

*T*or Claire

—M. D.

Much of the scientific material for this book is based on research by Dr. Scott Mori and Carol Gracie of the New York Botanical Garden. Many thanks for their support, encouragement, and friendship.

—M. R.

Here is the tropical rain forest.

Here is the rain

that drizzles and pours
and may fall every day
in this lush and wet world:
Here is the tropical rain forest.

*H*ere is the frog

who bathes in the rain

that drizzles and pours

and may fall every day

in this lush and wet world:

Here is the tropical rain forest.

*H*ere is the bromeliad

that shelters the frog

who bathes in the rain

that drizzles and pours

and may fall every day

in this lush and wet world:

Here is the tropical rain forest.

*H*ere is the tree,

which holds the bromeliad

that shelters the frog

who bathes in the rain

that drizzles and pours

and may fall every day

in this lush and wet world:

Here is the tropical rain forest.

Here is the sloth

that hangs from the tree,

which holds the bromeliad

that shelters the frog

who bathes in the rain

that drizzles and pours

and may fall every day

in this lush and wet world:

Here is the tropical rain forest.

*H*ere is the eagle

who hunts the sloth

that hangs from the tree,

which holds the bromeliad

that shelters the frog

who bathes in the rain

that drizzles and pours

and may fall every day

in this lush and wet world:

Here is the tropical rain forest.

*H*ere are the monkeys

that flee from the eagle

who hunts the sloth

that hangs from the tree,

which holds the bromeliad

that shelters the frog

who bathes in the rain

that drizzles and pours

and may fall every day

in this lush and wet world:

Here is the tropical rain forest.

*H*ere are the figs,

which are dropped by the monkeys

that flee from the eagle

who hunts the sloth

that hangs from the tree,

which holds the bromeliad

that shelters the frog

who bathes in the rain

that drizzles and pours

and may fall every day

in this lush and wet world:

Here is the tropical rain forest.

Here are the peccaries

that eat the figs,

which are dropped by the monkeys

that flee from the eagle

who hunts the sloth

that hangs from the tree,

which holds the bromeliad

that shelters the frog

who bathes in the rain

that drizzles and pours

and may fall every day

in this lush and wet world:

Here is the tropical rain forest.

Here is the jaguar

who stalks the peccaries

that eat the figs,

which are dropped by the monkeys

that flee from the eagle

who hunts the sloth

that hangs from the tree,

which holds the bromeliad

that shelters the frog

who bathes in the rain

that drizzles and pours

and may fall every day

in this lush and wet world:

Here is the tropical rain forest.

*H*ere is the caiman

that fights the jaguar

who stalks the peccaries

that eat the figs,

which are dropped by the monkeys

that flee from the eagle

who hunts the sloth

that hangs from the tree,

which holds the bromeliad

that shelters the frog

who bathes in the rain

that drizzles and pours

and may fall every day

in this lush and wet world:

Here is the tropical rain forest.

*H*ere is the river,

which is home to the caiman

that fights the jaguar

who stalks the peccaries

that eat the figs,

which are dropped by the monkeys

that flee from the eagle

who hunts the sloth

that hangs from the tree,

which holds the bromeliad

that shelters the frog

who bathes in the rain

that drizzles and pours

and may fall every day

in this lush and wet world:

Here is the tropical rain forest.

*H*ere is the rain

that fills the river,

which is home to the caiman

that fights the jaguar

who stalks the peccaries

that eat the figs,

which are dropped by the monkeys

that flee from the eagle

who hunts the sloth

that hangs from the tree,

which holds the bromeliad

that shelters the frog

who bathes in the rain

that drizzles and pours

and may fall every day

in this lush and wet world:

Here is the tropical rain forest.

The animals shown below live in the tropical rain forests of Central and South America. Tropical rain forests also exist in Africa and Southeast Asia and in other lands along the equator. Tropical rain forests are very rich in wildlife — half of the world's animal and plant species make their home there.

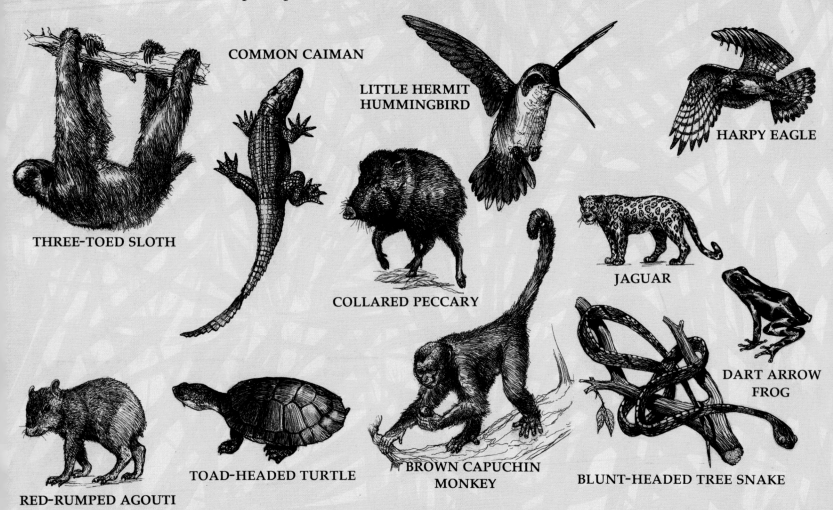

COMMON CAIMAN

LITTLE HERMIT
HUMMINGBIRD

HARPY EAGLE

THREE-TOED SLOTH

JAGUAR

COLLARED PECCARY

DART ARROW
FROG

TOAD-HEADED TURTLE

BROWN CAPUCHIN
MONKEY

BLUNT-HEADED TREE SNAKE

RED-RUMPED AGOUTI

Like many natural environments, tropical rain forests are threatened by human activities. If you would like to find out ways to help protect tropical rain forests, you can write to National Wildlife Federation, Division 811, 1400 16th Street, NW, Washington, DC, 20036.